That's
Wild!

™

MYsTerious Black Widows

by Peter Murray

sundance™

Sundance/Newbridge, LLC
33 Boston Post Road West
Suite 440
Marlborough, MA 01752
800-343-8204
www.sundancepub.com

Adapted from *Naturebooks,* published in 2003 by The Child's World®, Inc.
P.O. Box 326
Chanhassen, MN 55317-0326

Photo Credits: Front cover © Brian Kenney; p. 2 © Bill Beatty/Animals
Animals; p. 6 © Anthony Mercieca/Dembinsky Photo Assoc., Inc.; p. 9
© G. W. Willis/Animals Animals; p. 13 © Bill Johnson; pp. 17, 21 (inset)
© James H. Robinson/Animals Animals; p. 21 (main) © Doug Wechsler/
Animals Animals; pp. 22, 25, 26 © Robert and Linda Mitchell; p. 29
© Richard Shiell/Animals Animals; p. 30 © Karen Tweedy-Holmes/
Corbis; back cover, pp. 10, 14, 18 © TC Nature/Animals Animals

ISBN 978-0-7608-9344-9

Printed by Nordica International Ltd.
Manufactured in Guangzhou, China
April, 2011
Nordica Job#: 03-42-11
Sundance/Newbridge PO#: 226440

Contents

The attic is dark. Cobwebs are all over the place. You notice that some of the webs are neatly made. But others go every which way. On one of these sits a small spider. It is shiny and black. It is also dangerous.

It's a black widow!

The black widow's web is a messy, tangled shape.

2 ▶ Where Do Black Widows Live?

Black widows live in almost every state. They make their webs where they won't be bothered. They live **under rocks** and in wood piles. They live in dark corners of homes, too.

You might never know where these spiders are. They like to hide. That's because they are shy. They just want to be left alone. So *don't disturb their webs!*

This female black widow lives in an Arizona canyon.

3 ▸ What Are Black Widows?

Like all other spiders, black widows are **arachnids.** Arachnids have eight legs, and their body has two parts. Their mouth, eyes, brain, and stomach are in the front part. The back part contains their **heart.** Spiders make silk in this part, too. It comes out of their **spinnerets**.

Here you can see this female's spinnerets at the back of her body.

Who are you calling "itsy bitsy"?

Black widows don't all look the same. The female is about the size of a pea. She has a **red hourglass shape** on her belly. Usually, she hangs upside down from her web. The red shape can be seen then. It acts as **a warning** to others to keep away.

The male is a fourth the size of the female. He is usually brown in color. He also has orange, yellow, or white **stripes** on his back. His legs are slightly longer than a female's.

This male black widow is walking on a log.

13

The black widow waits for an insect to get caught in its web. It spins the **prey** in silk. Then the spider bites the prey with its fangs. The poison from its fangs makes the prey unable to move. Now the spider is ready to eat it. So it sucks the insect dry!

Females usually live in just one place. They live for about a year. Scientists studied one over the course of her life. She ate 1 caterpillar, 2 crickets, and 255 flies!

This female is feeding on an ant she trapped in her web.

6 ▶ Do Black Widows Live Alone?

A male lives for only a few months. As soon as he is big enough, he finds the web of a female. He then **touches her web.** This makes the web **vibrate,** or move. The male waits to see if she returns the vibrations. This will mean she is ready to mate. If she's not ready, she might just eat the male **for lunch!**

Here you can see how much larger a female is than a male.

The male leaves quickly after mating. If he doesn't, the female will **try to eat him.** (This is why these spiders are called black widows. Widows are females whose mate has died.) Sometimes the male brings the female a **dead insect.** He hopes that she will eat this gift. Then she will not be so hungry and want to eat him!

This male and female are getting ready to mate.

After mating, the female gets ready to lay her eggs. First she makes a **silk pouch.** This is called an **egg sac.** The sac is about as big as her body. She fills the sac with about 300 eggs. The eggs are usually yellow. A baby spider, or **spiderling,** will grow inside each egg.

Next the female covers the sac with silk. She puts it onto her web. Then she stays close so she can **protect her eggs.** A female can make up to nine egg sacs in three months.

Main Photo: This female is guarding her egg sacs.

Inset: Notice all the tiny eggs that are in an egg sac.

In a few weeks, a hole appears in each egg sac. This is where the **spiderlings** come out. They don't have any markings yet. They are light brown or white in color. They are also rubbery.

The mother watches them as they crawl out of the sac. If she is hungry, she will eat a few of them. The babies are hungry, too. Sometimes they eat each other!

This female is guarding her babies as they crawl out of the hole in the egg sac.

Each spiderling grows fast. Every few weeks, it gets **too big** for its own skin. So it has to **molt,** or shed its skin. To do this, it hangs from a strand of silk. It bends its body until its skin breaks open. Then it wriggles out from its old skin. The spider will molt many times before it reaches full size.

A baby turns gray or yellow after it first molts. Its abdomen looks orange. Each time that the spider molts, its skin gets darker. After the last molt, it has its adult colors.

These spiderlings could get eaten by their hungry mother.

Soon the spiderlings leave their mother. Some find a **dark corner** that is close by and build their first web. But most find something tall and climb to the top of it. Then the spider spins out a long strand of silk. The wind catches the strand and lifts the spider **into the air.** The spider is carried far away. When the spider lands, it finds a dark place to build its first web.

These spiderlings are almost ready to build their own webs.

Male black widows are harmless to people. But watch out for the female! One bite from her can make a person very sick. Most people will get better. But some have died from her bite.

This female has built her web in a quiet corner of a California home.

29

Some people think black widows are mean. They think black widows should be killed. But these spiders are really shy. They don't bite unless they are bothered. They even help people by eating lots of insects.

Black widows like to live in hidden places. Don't let one live under your bed, though! They are small. But they are dangerous. You don't want to mess with this spider!

This female is spinning her web at Zion National Park in Utah.

Glossary

arachnids animals that have eight legs and a body divided into two parts

egg sac a baglike holder some animals make to keep their eggs safe

molt to shed the outer layer of skin, fur, or feathers

prey animals that are eaten by other animals

spiderling a baby spider

spinnerets the body parts of a spider where silk comes out

vibrate to move from side to side rapidly

Index